A New Dimension

MICHAEL GREEN

A LION BOOK

Tring • Batavia • Sydney

Text copyright © 1988 Michael Green
This edition copyright © 1988 Lion Publishing

Published by
Lion Publishing plc
Icknield Way, Tring, Herts, England
ISBN 0 7459 1442 X
Lion Publishing Corporation
1705 Hubbard Avenue, Batavia, Illinois 60510, USA
ISBN 0 7459 1442 X
Albatross Books Pty Ltd
PO Box 320, Sutherland, NSW 2232, Australia
ISBN 0 86760 972 9

First edition 1981
published under the title *What is Christianity?*
Second edition 1985
published under the title *Lift-off to Faith*
This revised edition 1988

Bible quotations from *Good News Bible*, copyright
1966, 1971 and 1976 American Bible Society,
published by Bible Societies/Collins

Acknowledgments
Photograph on page 57 by Lion Publishing/David Townsend.
Photograph on page 61 by Hutchinson Picture Library.
All other photographs by ZEFA UK.

British Library Cataloguing in Publication Data
Green, Michael, 1930–
    A new dimension.—Rev. ed.
    1. Christian life
    I. Title   II. Green, Michael,
    Lift-off to faith
    248.4
    ISBN 0-7459-1442-X
    ISBN 0-86760-972-9 Australia

Library of Congress Cataloging-in-Publication Data
Green, Michael, 1930–
    A new dimension.
    Rev. ed. of: Lift-off to faith. 2nd ed. 1985.
    1. Christianity.   I. Green, Michael, 1930–   Lift-
    off to faith.   II. Title.
    BR121.2.G697 1988   200   87-35257
    ISBN 0-7459-1442-X

Printed and bound in Yugoslavia

CONTENTS

FASTEN YOUR SAFETY BELTS

The world in which we live has been shrunk to a 'global village' by modern communications and technology.

The New York businessman leaves John F. Kennedy Airport after breakfast, cruises at twice the speed of sound over the Atlantic, and arrives in London in time for lunch.

But what sort of world is it for most of its inhabitants? Is technology really going to solve the big questions facing humanity today?

And how can we understand ourselves – the race who people this planet? On the one hand we achieve scientific miracles. On the other hand we invent sickening cruelties and vices.

Every day television news blows our minds with stories of cruelty, suffering, guerrilla warfare, violence. Have we really advanced morally from the barbarism of ancient times?

Has Christianity a place in today's world?

If technology sidesteps our deeper questions, what sort of answers can we find in the Christian faith? Or is it a survival from our pre-scientific past? A superstition we have outgrown?

Satellites orbiting above the Earth transmit live television pictures around the globe. But has this instant communication drawn us any closer to people from other nations?

Western society is now largely secular. It is concerned with this world and unaware of any other. So too, increasingly, are the urban societies of Asia, Africa, Latin America. Many Arab countries are fast moving in the same direction, though it is exactly this development that militant Islamic leaders are now trying to reverse. In the 'socialist' blocs, religion of any sort is officially scorned or actively persecuted.

But this is not the whole picture. There is strong evidence that worldwide Christianity is in a phase of advance, despite its local decline in the West.

Membership of churches in many third-world countries is growing astonishingly fast. It has been claimed for the whole of Africa south of the Sahara that if conversions continue at the present rate the whole region will be Christian by the year 2000.

Many young people across the world are finding that Christianity has something to say to them for the 1990s. It may not fit comfortably in the modern world. True Christianity has never been comfortable. But it talks about real issues from a radical standpoint.

In an age of empty slogans and a massive identity crisis, the Christian promise of new life in Christ is felt by many to be a breath of fresh air.

GOD AT WORK

Is life just a confused chaos of human activity, happiness, misery, life, death? Or is there something to it? Is there something going on here that makes sense?

Christians believe that God is at work in the world. He made it in the first place. But he did not simply go away and leave everything to its own devices. Not even a human creator would do that. God is involved in his world. He 'holds it together'.

No one has ever seen God. We may find the signs of his activity in the world hard to spot. But (as the apostle Paul wrote) 'ever since God created the world, his invisible qualities, both his eternal power and his divine nature, have been clearly seen; they are perceived in the things that God has made.'

God is at work in the world. He is 'general manager' of the whole outfit.

Nothing – not even the dark side of life – happens without God's permission.

This raises many questions. How can a good God allow suffering and evil? There is so much we do not understand . . . now. But Christians see a greater purpose in God's plan. The final stage of the world will provide a vantage-point from which all today's joy and pain will be seen in their true meaning.

We find it easier to see God at work through people. In this way he is involved intimately, personally, in every part of life.

Creativity in the arts, technical skill in complex processes, the patient care of surgeons in India, the practical love shown in famine relief in Ethiopia, the maximizing of earth's resources through agriculture schemes in Africa . . . all these remind us that God is creative, and he carries on creating through the skill he has given us.

To see this gives a boost to developing our creative gifts. It can make our daily job worthwhile.

Healing diseased bodies and shattered lives, drawing a parched earth back to productive life . . . these are things everyone recognizes as good.

Many Christians get involved in such action. But God is equally at work in these ways through many others who do not see their work as his . . .

. . . yet.

A CREEPING SICKNESS

Despite all the signs of God at work in the world, it is still in a mess.

• There is appalling inequality between rich and poor nations. In 1983 the national income for each person in the United States was $9,600, in China $510, in India $170.

• A massive population explosion is on the way. By the year 2000 there will be twice as many mouths to feed as there were in 1950. They increase at 210,000 a day – starvation affects more and more of mankind.

• The world is running short not only of food but of oil and energy. The age of abundance is over, and yet the West continues in careless extravagance.

• The air, the land and the waters of the earth are being ruined. Dumping radioactive waste in the sea is just one of the ways we are poisoning the environment for future generations.

• Families are breaking up, with great misery and hurt. One marriage in three collapses.

• The crime rate all over the world is accelerating with terrifying rapidity. It is an age of violence and brutality such as the world has never seen. It is the age of concentration camps, of the most exquisite forms of torture, of genocide.

Leonardo da Vinci suppressed his invention of the submarine, he tells us, 'because of the evil nature of man. They would use it to practise assassinations at the bottom of the sea.'

He had put his finger on the heart of our problem: the evil nature of human beings.

'What's wrong with the world? I am,' said a famous man of letters.

Of course, if you put that to the man in the street he will tell you: 'I've never done anyone any harm.' 'I'm all right.' 'I'm as good as people who go to church.'

But Christianity will have none of it. The Christian faith is unashamedly a rescue religion. That is why so many respectable people will have nothing to do with it. The Bible proclaims that we are *not* all right. The world is in a mess, and each individual life is in a mess.

'Who can understand the human heart?' asked the prophet Jeremiah. 'There is nothing else so deceitful; it is too sick to be healed.'

Jesus himself tells us something crucial – something that we are painfully having to rediscover today. Will more education or more social welfare put us right? Or is it 'the system'? Change the system and all will be right . . .

No, said Jesus. For 'from our heart come the evil ideas which lead us to kill, commit adultery, and do other immoral things; to rob, lie, and slander others.'

The fault lies not in our stars but in ourselves. The 'human disease' of self-centredness is nothing short of fatal.

You must have seen a tree throttled by ivy. It is a sad sight. A tree is such a strong, beautiful, living thing. And we feel it ought never to succumb to the insignificant tentacles climbing up it.

But ivy is like a creeping sickness. Look how it starts: so pale, and frail, and innocent-looking. But it grows. It increases its hold, shuts out the light and air, and eventually strangles the life out of the tree.

That is very like the effect on us of the disease the Bible calls sin. We were made to be great – the crown of God's creation. But sin spoils it all.

'Whoever commits sin becomes a slave of sin,' said Jesus.

'I do not understand what I do; for I don't do what I would like to do, but instead I do what I hate . . . What an unhappy man i am! Who will rescue me?' cried the apostle Paul. 'Sin pays its customers; the wage is death.'

This is all very unflattering for a generation which thinks it is the greatest. But it is a true analysis, however humiliating. It means that we need two things above all:
• Forgiveness for the mess we have made of our world and of our lives;
• A power beyond our own to set us free.

BATTLE FOR THE MIND

This used to be called the age of the hidden persuaders. The advertisers, TV, films, newspapers – these were the weapons in the battle for the mind.

But the persuaders are no longer hidden. They are strident. Listen to the parrot cries at party political conferences in the West. Listen to the chants of guerrillas in the African bush. Watch the rape of the minds in Russia, China and many other countries. Propaganda . . . distortion . . . brainwashing. The battle for the mind is on.

Thousands fanatically support political and religious causes. They claim to be following the truth. But how do we know what is truth and what fiction?

The Roman emperors calculated that if they provided bread and circuses for the masses they could manipulate people very much as they pleased. Today we look to the welfare state for the bread, pop music and football for the circuses, and the result can be much the same.

There are plenty of manipulators of the mind in the field today. They are out to produce programmed men and women.

Is Christianity just another of the competing, manipulative ideologies in our world? Yet another opiate to dull the pain of daily life? Or does it rightly claim to be true, to be a faith to live by, and a challenge to the manipulators of ideas?

I would want to see these conditions fulfilled in any faith claiming my allegiance for today:

• It must be true. In the long run people will not be satisfied by a fraud or a lie. Jesus Christ claimed to show the truth about God and humanity; indeed, to be the truth. Down the ages, his claim has worn well.

• It must be relevant. If it makes no difference to the lives of ordinary people, it is no good. It has got to enrich the quality of life. Christianity makes precisely that claim. Jesus said, 'I have come that you may have life – life in all its fulness.'

• It must be big enough to meet many needs. It must not be petty or individualistic, but wide enough in its scope and influence to transform national and international relationships, to affect medicine, education, ecology, peace and industrial relations. Despite all the failures of churches and individual Christians Jesus Christ has continued to have that effect on the world. Right up to today.

• It must have universal appeal. If a faith appeals to one

segment of society alone, or one race alone, then it is too small and too narrow for me. But Jesus is the man for all seasons and for all races. He has drawn to himself blacks and whites, rich and poor, clever and simple, Eskimos and Arabs, communists and capitalists from all over the world. It is happening now, as people all over the world are converted to Christianity at a rate of 60,000 a day. And always his impetus has been towards unity, love and development.

● It must be big enough to embrace death. A faith to live by is a poor thing if it is not also a faith to die by. Jesus is the only world leader who claims to have conquered death. Hundreds of millions believe that claim. Because Jesus rose from the grave that first Easter Day, his followers can face death without fear.

Jesus Christ does not come to us as a hidden persuader or a ruthless dictator. He does not want conformist minds and programmed people. He invites us to consider his claims, to face up to his challenge . . . and then make a free choice about following him.

WHAT DO WE KNOW ABOUT JESUS?

A century ago there was a lot of talk suggesting that Jesus never existed. 'Just another dying-and-rising god,' they said, 'like Greek mythology.' At much the same time Karl Marx was falling under the influence of a theology professor called Bruno Bauer who was sacked for heresy. He maintained that the Jesus story was dreamed up late in the second century. This bizarre view is still official Communist teaching. And today there are plenty of people who say Jesus was a visitor from outer space in a UFO!

All such views are doomed to failure. Why? Because they ignore the good historical evidence for Jesus of Nazareth.

● First, you have the accounts of the life of Jesus, the Gospels, and the letters of the New Testament – a completely new literary explosion brought about by Jesus.

● Second, there is evidence from Roman historians for Jesus' existence, his unusual birth, his execution by crucifixion under Pontius Pilate, who governed the turbulent province of Judea from AD26 to AD36.

● Third, there are archaeological remains which show that people were worshipping Jesus in Palestine and Italy by the middle of the first century.

● Fourth, ancient Jewish testimony makes clear allusions to his unusual birth, his death on the cross, his miracles, his divine claims and the birth of the church. Both Jewish and Roman evidence is hostile to Christians. Therefore its testimony is all the more valuable, and it chimes in closely with what the Gospels tell us.

And what do the Gospels teach? They tell us that Jesus was

more than simply the carpenter of Nazareth; more than a famous rabbi; more even than the best of men. But, on the other hand, they never tell us that he was just God Almighty dressed up as a human being.

No, they struggle at the boundaries of language to express their conviction that in Jesus Christ God has shown us what he is like, within the terms of a human life. Not that Jesus was all of God that there is; he constantly spoke of his 'heavenly Father'. Rather, that he is the tip of the iceberg of God, and the rest of the iceberg is all of a piece with the part we can see.

This is what astounded and thrilled those Jews who became the first Christian believers. Living cheek by jowl with Jesus for three years persuaded them that he was no mere man, but that God himself had cared enough to come and seek us out in the person of Jesus.

If we matter that much to God, no wonder their message became known as 'godspel': good news.

A NEW DIMENSION

The first recorded words of Jesus electrified his hearers.

'The moment of opportunity has dawned. God's kingdom is at hand. Change your attitudes, and believe the good news!'

The 'kingdom of God' featured a great deal in his teaching. He was always talking about it. But what is it?

By 'the kingdom of God', Jesus meant a whole new start for a world gone wrong. Instead of being dominated by selfishness, men and women would welcome God's rule in their lives. Jesus introduced this kingly rule in a new way; because he, alone of all men, fully obeyed God's will throughout his life. He lived out the kingdom of God which he proclaimed. He demonstrated what a life in touch with God at every point would look like.

He was the kingdom in person.
• He showed us what the ideal king is like – perfect, living, challenging, incorruptible.
• He showed us what the ideal subject is like – obedient, full of faith, loyal even up to death.

In other words, if you want to know what God is like, look at Jesus. There you see the perfection of God lived out without distortion in a human life. And if you want to know what people are meant to be like, look at Jesus. There you see in clear focus the full range of human virtues in a life of total dependence on God.

The way to enter this kingdom is very costly, and yet very simple. It means:

- First a total change of priorities and direction, or repentance.
- And then trust in and commitment to Jesus Christ, or faith.

The way to live in the kingdom is equally costly yet simple. It means saying yes to God's offer to put within us a new life, the life of the kingdom.

The result will be that we begin to try and please him in everything. We get into the habit of asking ourselves, 'How would Jesus have handled this situation?', and acting accordingly. What is more, we begin to discover in experience the power he gives to make that sort of living possible. It is a radically new life.

During the 1970s the eyes of the world were focused on Uganda and the violent rule of their president, Idi Amin. The new dimension, the 'kingdom dimension', was seen very clearly in the terrible situation in which hundreds of thousands of Ugandans, most of them Christian believers, were slaughtered by Amin.

One of these men was Archbishop Janani Luwum, whom I knew well. Gently and firmly he opposed the tyranny of General Amin. Graciously he remonstrated with him, in the name of God and of justice.

When Amin would not listen he had Janani killed.

As he was led to the torture chamber he and another tortured prisoner prayed for the President.

That is the life of the kingdom.

When Amin refused to release the bullet-ridden body,

thousands broke a government ban and held a funeral service outside the cathedral in Kampala – with an empty grave. They sang the song of the East African revival, and the preacher spoke on these words of the New Testament: 'He is not here, he is risen.'

That is the life of the kingdom.

And Janani was not unique. His fellow-bishop, Festo Kivengere, escaped with his life by a hair's breadth – and then wrote a book called *I Love Idi Amin*.

That is the life of the kingdom.

When men live and die like that, the words of Jesus are fulfilled quite literally: 'Blessed are the meek, for they shall inherit the earth.'

That is the life of the kingdom.

FAMILIES NEED FATHERS

In the West two things are happening. Families are breaking up. And the children are getting into trouble.

Absentee fathers lead to delinquency. The family matters – and families need fathers.

Much of Jesus' teaching is about God the Father. He said God was his Father. He said God could be our Father. And that immediately raises some questions.

Jesus taught that God is like a parent and we his children. He cares for us and continues to love us – even when we fail.

'Yes, I believe in God. Something must have started the world off.'

Many people think like this, and it makes sense. But Jesus says this is a very inadequate picture of God. He is a person, not a thing. He is Father. Father in the sense that he gave life to the world and us. Father in the sense that he loves the world and us.

'I can't believe God is like my old man.'

Fair enough. Our human fathers often leave much to be desired. The Bible says that all fatherhood derives from God, but it is often a grossly distorted copy. All the same, we have some idea of what a real father would be like: strong, loving, able to guide and teach and discipline us. Jesus taught that God was like that.

'Yes, but surely we are all children of God?'

Here the Bible says an emphatic 'No' – except in the sense that we are all God's creation. You see, sons resemble their fathers. And we do not resemble God. We don't live like him or love like him. Indeed, most of the time we are strangers to him, if not active rebels against him.

Jesus taught that there was only one real Son of God. Himself. He coined a new word for it – 'Abba'. It means 'Daddy'. Nobody had ever dared to call God that before Jesus. Nobody had the right to do so.

But Jesus did. He claimed time and again that God was his Abba, his 'dear Father'. In other words, if you wanted to know what the Father was like, you could get a very good idea from the Son. He shared his Father's character, and life, and love.

But the really astonishing thing is that this perfect Son of the heavenly Father offers us a share in the family life.

'Jesus came to his own world, but his own people did not receive him.' That is a very fair summary of what happened. But wait . . . 'Some, however, *did* receive him and believed in him; so he gave them the right to become sons of God.'

That's what a Christian is: a child of God.

The Christian has his Father to protect, to guide, to give him strength. He loves the Father, wants to please him, delights in being with him and talking to him.

You don't become a child of God by the accident of birth.

You don't become a child of God by trying hard to be good.

You don't become a child of God just by being baptized or confrrmed.

You become a son of God when you welcome the Son of God into your life. You then get adopted into God's family. And you never get thrown out. That is what a Christian is, a child of God. It is hardly surprising that crowds flocked to Jesus to hear more.

COSMIC WARFARE

There's a war on.

As a matter of fact, there are a lot of wars going on at this very minute. There have been nearly a hundred since World War Two.

But there is one war which has been going on ever since there have been people on earth. The war between good and evil, between God and Satan.

And before you write that off as old-fashioned rubbish, pause and think. Why is it that children never need to be taught to lie and hate and rebel? Why is it that the greatest wars in this century have broken out between the best educated, most advanced societies with the best standards of living?

Because there is a war on.

Part of our problem is other people. Their influence drags us down. We are reluctant to stand up for what we know is right, and be different. The Bible calls this powerful pressure 'the world'.

Part of our problem is ourselves. There seems to be a traitor in the camp. We see what is right; we approve of it; but we often do the opposite. The Bible calls this inner weakness 'the flesh'.

And part of our trouble is Satan. Not some fun figure with cloven hooves and a forked tail. But an angel who rebelled against God and wants to involve the whole world in his rebellion. The Bible calls this evil spirit 'the devil'.

That is why we find it so hard even to live up to our own indifferent standards. There is a great spiritual force of evil seducing us away from the right path, and he uses the pressures of society and our own weakness to drag us down.

The world . . . the flesh . . . the devil . . . all these oppose us.

Nobody can prove that this account of the world is true. But it is certainly what the Bible teaches. And it does make sense. It ties up with our experience of life.

In Northern Ireland there has been a war on for years. But if you go to Ireland you will very seldom see actual street warfare. Generally all seems peaceful and friendly. Life goes on as usual. But there is a war on all the same.

Hidden agents wait for the right moment to strike. Innocent people are involved in the disasters. Attack comes when you least expect it. There is a war on.

Equally certainly there is a spiritual war going on beneath the surface of life. Hence the disease, the hate, the wars, the sins of individuals and society. And God cares.

He cares so much that he came to our world to do something about the sorry mess. The Bible puts it like this: 'The Son of God appeared for this very reason, to destroy what the devil had done.'

AN ASTOUNDING CLAIM

To talk about Jesus as the Son of God begs the questions: 'Who was he?' 'Was he the Son of God?' Lots of people make claims. They need checking out. Do they match up in experience?

In the 1970s Evel Knievel was the highest-paid entertainer in the world. He specialized in promising to do the most sensational things. And he broke almost every bone in his body failing to keep all his promises.

He had a great idea in 1974. He was going to jump the Snake Canyon on a rocket-assisted motorcycle. It is over 500 metres wide, and the rocket would launch a parachute with him attached. He would make 30 million dollars through television and tickets. It would be an amazing spectacle.

The trouble was he did not make good his claims. His rocket fired, his parachute opened, but he only got as far as the floor of the Canyon.

The difference with Jesus was just this. He did make good his claims, all along the line.
• He claimed to have the power to heal sick people at will – and he proved it by total success in every type of healing.
• He claimed to have the power to forgive sins – something only God can do. 'Your sins are forgiven you,' he said to a paralyzed man – and proved his authority by healing him.
• He claimed to be the only one who could reveal God to people and bring people to God – and he has been doing it ever since.

- He claimed that he and his Father were one, and that he was the way, the truth and the life for all humanity. He made good this claim by the quality of life he lived.
- He claimed to be the long-awaited Suffering Servant of God, who would take away the sins of the world – and he proved it by dying on the cross.
- He claimed that it would be proper for men and women to worship him – and Thomas, his once sceptical disciple, fell down at his feet confessing 'My Lord and my God'.
- He claimed that he would one day be entrusted with the judgment of every man, woman and child in the universe, and that their destiny for all eternity would be determined by their relation to himself – and one day we will discover for ourselves whether that claim is true or not.
- He claimed that he would be put to death on a cross and rise to life again on the third day. It happened, and that is one of the strongest reasons why we can believe he really is the Son of God.

The apostle Paul wrote: 'Jesus was descended from David physically. But he was shown to be the Son of God by the resurrection from the dead.'

FOLLOW ME

Imagine you are on holiday in the Swiss Alps. It is one thing to like mountains. Or admire them or read books about them. It is quite another thing to climb them, even roped to an expert.

If you are going to try to climb a mountain like the Eiger, you must . . .
- Trust your guide completely,
- Listen to his commands and obey them at once,
- Be roped to him and to others on the climb.

There is no other way you can hope to reach the top . . .

This is the sort of relationship Jesus Christ expects of his disciples. He did not advise people to listen to his teaching. He commanded them to follow him.

'As Jesus walked along the shore of Lake Galilee, he saw two fishermen, Simon and his brother Andrew, catching fish with a net. Jesus said to them, "Come with me."'

This is just where the teaching of Jesus is so different from the other great teachers of the world. They all pointed to some side of the truth and said 'Follow that'. He claimed to be the truth and said 'Follow me'.

Others before him had taught about living a good life. Jesus claimed that he was God's life come into the midst of humanity. It made sense to invite people to share that life. How? By coming to follow him.

Many religious leaders had concerned themselves with the way to God. The difference with Jesus was that he claimed

to be that way to God. No one could discover God as Father except through him. No wonder he invited them to follow him.

'I am the way, the truth, and the life,' he said. 'No one goes to the Father except by me.' That is why he told people that they must follow him.

It is hardly surprising that these claims made him a threat to the Jewish leaders. This man was different . . .

The first Christians liked to call themselves 'followers of the Way'. They had a personal link of allegiance to Jesus.

It is important to be clear about this, for all sorts of people think they are Christians who would not say they had any personal link with Jesus Christ. They say
- 'I live a decent life.'
- 'I agree with the teaching of Jesus.'
- 'I go to church.'

But that does not make a person a Christian. Jesus calls each of us personally to follow him.

Being a Christian means deciding to follow and to rely on God.

A CHANGE OF DIRECTION

At the heart of the teaching of Jesus is the challenge to change the whole direction of our lives. This seems very strange to us these days. It is more common to believe that it does not really matter which route you choose – they all take you to the top of the mountain.

Jesus says that they do not.

I once came across this remarkable signpost in the heart of rural Wales. One finger reads 'Llanwrthwl 4½', and the other, directly opposite, reads precisely the same. It does not matter which way you go. You land up at Llanwrthwl.

But you do not land up in the family of God by heading off in any direction you please. That is the sure way to go astray.

According to Jesus you need to repent and believe.

'Repentance' does not mean shedding crocodile tears over past failures. To repent means:
• To change your attitudes to God, to what is wrong, to other people.
• To allow God to make changes in your life that are overdue but which you never got round to.
• To stop putting yourself first, and start putting God first.

God's call for repentance is nothing short of a take-over bid. It tells us that there is one way to God. Jesus is that one way. And to follow him means turning away from other paths and committing yourself to his.

Repentance was one requirement which Jesus never tired of stressing.

The other one was belief or 'faith'.

Faith does not mean believing what you know is not true.

Faith does not mean the last resort when things are black.

Faith does not mean agreeing with something in your mind while it makes no difference whatever to your life.

Faith means believing about somebody in such a way that you believe in them. If you are a trapeze artist, you believe that the other trapeze artist is reliable. You believe he can take your weight.

By itself, of course, that does not move you one inch from the safety of your bar.

But it does give you good grounds for committing yourself to that leap through the air which results in a very sharp change of direction.

When you do that, you show that you really believe in the other person. You quite literally bet your life on his reliability. You entrust your whole self and your future to him. That is what the Bible means by faith. It is not blind. Jesus Christ is every bit as reliable as the trapeze artist – far more so, in fact.

Some people have called this the leap of faith. That is what it is. But it is not blind faith. It is an act of commitment, leading to a life of relationship. Repentance and faith make that change of direction without which it is impossible to follow Jesus.

But I do not actually believe in him in the full sense he was calling for, until I leave the security of my perch, whatever it happens to be, and bet my whole life on his faithfulness.

A trapeze artist has to trust the other members of the team. God asks us to place the same trust in him.

FREEDOM TO FIND YOURSELF

We all wear masks. There is the mask of the business man, the glamour girl, the soldier, the diplomat. We know what exterior to expect from each of them.

The smooth smile of the society hostess, the quick joke of the comedian, the cool apology of the tradesman, the bland calm of the clergyman – masks, all of them.

And inside?

One of the marvellous things that Jesus Christ did for everyone who came to follow him was to remove their masks. He insisted that they did not need to wear them any more. There was no reason to go on pretending.

For God himself had declared them accepted.

Once people realize that, once they come to feel it deep inside them, it brings the most profound liberation.

At last they are free to find themselves . . . and be themselves. Every movement worthy of the name offers freedom these days. It is a very fashionable word. Yet it is obvious that much of the freedom is in fact a new bondage. We tend to exchange one set of rules, one set of masters for another. We are still in bondage.

What of the freedom Jesus Christ offers?

Quite simply, it is the freedom to be the self that God intended us to be when he made us. That freedom has got spoiled by a variety of forces, but most profoundly of all by the sin which has put shackles on all our lives.

'Not me!' you say? That is just what the Jews said when Jesus first declared his offer of freedom. They were still wearing masks, still playing games. And gently Jesus removed the mask, and told them:

'Whoever does wrong becomes the slave of wrong.'

That is true, and depressing. That is why we wear masks to shut the unwelcome fact away.

But Jesus continued:

'If the Son sets you free, then you will be really free.'

That is true, too. And wonderfully liberating. Set free at last from the inner grip of constant failure. Released at last to be myself. I no longer need to pretend. God has seen the worst about me and still declares me accepted. Why need I pretend to others that I am any different from what I am?
• Christian freedom liberates a person from the crippling sense of guilt. God has dealt with all that through Jesus Christ and his death.
• Christian freedom liberates a person from being dominated by what 'they' think or expect. That person is free to be himself, the self God made him or her to be.
• Christian freedom sets a person free from constant defeat by bad habits and inadequacies. Released by the Son of God, we begin to taste real moral freedom.
• Christian freedom means we can be honest with each other about our failures, knowing not only that others have them too, but that God accepts us despite them.
• Christian freedom liberates us from bondage to a set of rules, be they new ones or old. It is the freedom to please a living person – Jesus Christ. That aim begins to dominate our motives and change our lives.

Many Christians never realize the freedom that is their

birthright. But others progressively do. And all may. For the offer of Jesus Christ stands:

'If the Son sets you free, then you will be really free.'

A DEATH THAT ACHIEVED EVERYTHING

One of the most amazing things about Jesus Christ is that his death is even more important than his life.

In most biographies a person's death is alluded to briefly in the last chapter. In the Gospels the death of Jesus is central. Nearly half of what is written in the Gospels relates to it in some way or another. Why?

The cross is the mark of Christianity. You find it around people's necks. You find it in their churches. Not a book – to remind you of Christ's Sermon on the Mount, say – but a cross to remind you of Christ's terrible death. Why?

His death was a martyr's death: Jesus was hounded to crucifixion for the sake of the unpalatable truth he taught – like lots of others down history.

His death was a sacrificial death: he went to it willingly, making the supreme sacrifice – like lots of others down history. But what made Jesus' death special? Quite simply, the fact of who he was. This was no mere dying. This was God in our midst. This is what makes the death of Jesus so special.

And here is what it tells us about God:
• He cares about us. Sometimes people say, 'Why does God seem so far away?' He may seem it, but he isn't. He came to our world, lived our human life and died as we must die – but in agony far worse than most of us have to undergo. God cares about us. He is not that vague 'Something' which started the world off and then left us to

get on with it. He cares so much that he came. He cares so much that he died.

• He understands our suffering. Sometimes people say 'Why does God allow it?' Or 'Why doesn't God do something about the suffering in the world?' He has!

Nobody can give a full explanation of the pain and suffering that spoils our world and our lives. The Bible teaches that it is somehow linked with human disobedience. We have gone off God's track, and inevitably there is chaos, painful chaos, as a result.

But Christianity gives a more satisfactory account of suffering than you can find anywhere else. Stoicism says 'Grin and bear it'. Buddhism says 'It is all an illusion'. Hinduism says 'It will give you a better reincarnation'. Christianity says, 'God has not explained it fully. But he has come to share it.'

Isn't that what we want when we are suffering in hospital? Not a long lecture on the causes of our pain, but someone to come alongside, and take our hand? The cross shows that God is like that. He is the suffering God. He understands human suffering – from the inside.

• He paid our debts. This is the deepest thing that the cross of Christ shows us. When Jesus died, he cried out 'Finished!' or 'The debt is paid!' It is as if all our wrong thoughts and words and deeds, all the flaws in our character, were one gigantic bill which we owed to the perfect, holy, loving God. He was so holy that he could not pretend it did not matter. He was so loving that he could not let it cut us off from him for ever.

So he acted. He allowed our guilt to crush him on the cross. He took our sin down into death.

'Christ himself carried our sins in his body to the cross.'

'For Christ died for sins once and for all, a good man on behalf of sinners, in order to lead us to God.'

'He cancelled the unfavourable record of our debts with its binding rules and did away with it completely by nailing it to the cross.'

In ways like this the New Testament writers wrestle to explain what Jesus achieved when he died on the cross.

Because he, the innocent one, took our filthy guilt upon himself, anyone who puts his trust in him is accepted by God – free from sin. Because he took responsibility in his death for the sins of the whole world, his cross divides people. It is both an assurance and a threat.

It is an assurance if we turn to him, acknowledging our faults and recognizing that he has put them away for ever: we can be, as the New Testament puts it, 'acquitted' – forgiven for all our sins.

It is a threat if we decline to turn to him, assuming we are all right as we are. The cross says we are not all right, and that it cost the agonies of a cruel death to put us in the right with him.

That's why the cross takes us to the heart of Christianity.

It is the death that achieved everything.

FLASHBACK

Jesus was a Jew.

When you see prosperous Jews in New York . . .

When you see inventive Jews in Israel . . .

When you hear of persecuted Jews in Hitler's gas chambers, or Siberian prisons . . .

. . . you are being confronted by one of God's great marvels.
- A people sprung from one man who believed and obeyed God – Abraham.
- A people 4,000 years old.
- A people who have retained their national identity throughout nearly 3,000 years of dispersion over the face of the globe.
- A people who have had no national home, no fatherland, between AD135 when they were kicked out of Palestine and 1948 when they secured a partial return.

The people into which Jesus was born.

God's chosen people, Israel.

In these days of equality, words like 'chosen people' make us angry. But there is no need for us to feel like that.

God did not choose Israel because they were better than anyone else. He did not choose them because they had done something to deserve it. Nor was there any favouritism about it. He chose them for a purpose. Just as a golfer might choose a club, or a pilot choose a plane.

It was like this.

God made a world that was perfect in every way. People were perfect too. And that perfection included their relationship with God. Men and women enjoyed God's love and shared their lives with him.

But very early in the story, people chose the selfish way, and turned their backs on God. They have been doing so ever since. So God, being the loving God he is, set out on a rescue operation. And the twelve tribes of Israel became the focus of his activity. Through this nation he would one day restore the knowledge of himself through the entire globe.

Their story is the story of the Old Testament. It is a story of failure and success, of disobedience and faith, of commoners and kings, shepherds and prophets. It is a story of the gradual conviction that there is one God alone in all the world, that they were his people bound to him by a sacred agreement and pledged to loyalty and obedience.

They also came to recognize that God is a holy God who cannot bear wickedness in his people. And when he comes in judgment, the guilty must die. This was a lesson which burnt itself deeply into the people and two great factors came to dominate their personal, social and national life.
• One was the Law, originally given through Moses, which regulated almost every aspect of life, and showed how God intended them to live.
• The other was the sacrificial system. Every morning and every evening there were sacrifices in the temple at Jerusalem. Every Day of Atonement there was a great sacrifice involving the whole nation. Sin was confessed, and the people's guilt was passed on to a victim – normally a

lamb or goat – by the high priest laying his hands on its head.

You could say that all this shedding of blood through sacrifices was a revolting waste. So it would have been, had it not pointed forward to something much greater. It was God's powerful way of teaching his people that his holiness simply cannot co-exist with evil. Death – separation from God – *has* to follow sin.

But the Old Testament was at pains to teach Israel that God has provided a way of escape. That way was to be by the death of none other than his own Son, Jesus Christ. It was paid in full, on the cross. And it was to this that the sacrificial system and the Passover looked forward.

Rescue comes through sacrifice, and by no other way.

That is the lesson Israel learnt during the twenty centuries before the coming of Christ.

WAITING FOR A LIBERATOR

There is a remarkable forward look in the religion of Israel. They had a system of animal sacrifices, but they knew in their hearts that the blood of goats and lambs could never take away sins.

They looked forward . . .

Prophecy was an outstanding feature among the Jews. God would raise up men to speak his will to the people, and also to lift their hearts to what God was going to do in the future.

It is not surprising, therefore, that when we come to Jesus we find him fulfilling so many forward pointers, or prophecies, of the Old Testament.

• The prophets had spoken of the 'new deal' or new covenant which would replace the old agreement between God and Israel which the people broke time and again. Jesus said he would inaugurate this 'new deal' by shedding his own blood on the cross, and he gave his followers the Holy Communion (or Eucharist or Lord's Supper) to imprint the memory of his sacrifice on the minds of every generation.

• The prophets had spoken of a king who would sit on King David's throne and reign in righteousness, and whose kingdom would be without frontiers. Jesus came announcing the arrival of that kingdom, and it has been growing ever since, so that now it literally spans the whole world.

• The prophets had spoken of the day when God would send his perfect servant to Israel, who would carry out his will in every detail, and gladly bear all the suffering involved. That famous verse, immortalized in Handel's *Messiah*, refers to this suffering servant:

'All we like sheep have gone astray. We have turned every one to his own way. And the Lord has laid on him (the suffering servant) the iniquity of us all.'

Jesus promised to fulfil that destiny of the suffering servant of God. And he did – on the cross. This is how his friend and follower Peter described the fulfilment of that old prophecy:

'Christ carried our sins in his body to the cross.'

'Christ died for sins once and for all . . . in order to lead us to God.'

Refugees, fleeing in the face of war, know the terrible bondage they are in. They know there is a better country, where freedom and justice are to be found. They are waiting, longing for a day of liberation.

And in the days of Herod, petty King of Judea, the Liberator was born. Not at all as they expected, with trumpets and armies and political success. That is not God's way. He chose an unmarried girl to be the mother of his Liberator. He chose a stable, not a palace. And Jesus worked as a carpenter, not a prince. But he went on to teach as no man ever taught. And he went on to die as a ransom for many.

In that death he proved he was no political Liberator, wheeling and dealing for the success of his schemes. To the Jews, death meant failure; worse, death on a cross meant the curse of God.

But if he bore the curse of God, it was our curse, borne so that we should never have to bear it. And out of 'political failure' came spiritual freedom for millions.

Such is the Liberator Israel longed for. And so does the rest of humanity.

Caught in a burning building and waiting for a liberator! The Bible describes how Christ came to free us from the destructive element within each one of us.

NEW LIFE, NEW POWER

The cross of Jesus was not the end of him.

If it had been, we could have been excused for thinking that God did not care.

If it had been, we could rightly have supposed that suffering has no purpose.

If it had been, we could rightly suppose that 'Finished!' was the cry of defeat, not of victory. And we would certainly have no assurance of forgiveness.

But the whole New Testament resounds with the echo of the resurrection of Jesus Christ. The resurrection started the Christian movement off, changing a bunch of terrified men into a task force. The resurrection spelt power, the power of God in our world. It was something utterly new.

But did it happen?
• Yes, it happened. The tomb was empty on the third day. Just the grave-clothes were left as they had been, wrapped round the body. Like the chrysalis case when the butterfly has emerged.
• Yes, it happened. His enemies could not deny it. His followers were ecstatic about it. And they spread like wildfire.
• Yes, it happened. He kept appearing to different people in different situations for six weeks, assuring them he was alive and commissioning them to go and tell the good news all over the world.
• Yes, it happened all right. You could not explain the change in the day of worship from Saturday to Sunday if it

had not. You could not explain the rise of the Christian movement if it had not. You could not explain its power to change lives if it had not.

Power to change lives. That's what the resurrection means. In our generation we have seen an utterly new dimension to power. Power to launch rockets to the moon and the stars. Undreamed of new power. But nothing compared with the power of the resurrection, which unlocked the gates of death – fast shut since the death of the first man.

What kind of power do we mean?

We don't like the idea of power too much. We remember that all power tends to corrupt. We dislike the overtones of power over other people.

But the power of the risen Christ is quite different.
• It is the power to go straight. I think of the alcoholic, the compulsive gambler, the dishonest businessman – utterly changed once they come in touch with the power of the risen Christ.
• It is the power to unite them in love. I think of places where Jews and Arabs, folk from Northern and Southern Ireland, from the black and white communities in South Africa, now live not in hatred but in love and mutual service. It is only the power of Jesus Christ, risen from the dead, which can achieve that miracle.
• It is the power to face death with triumph. More Christians have been martyred in this generation than in any previous one. And they have gone to their deaths with calm, with love and with hymns of praise. They know that not even death can sever them from the living Christ.
• It is the power to change society. Education, medicine, liberation throughout the world have been brought about

more by the gospel of the risen Christ than by any other agency.

This power is not, I repeat *not*, Christians trying to be good!

The hang glider doesn't try to fly and conquer the downward pull of gravity. He simply trusts himself to a power far greater than his own: the power of the air currents to give him lift.

That is what the Christian does. He entrusts himself to the power of the risen Christ, and in that power he rises to heights he could never otherwise have reached. He has found a new life with Christ. And that life means a new power.

THE BURNING MEN

All the preparation for the coming of Jesus took place in the Jewish nation. Jesus lived, taught, died and rose again, all within the Jewish homeland. So when did Christianity break out from its Jewish limits and become a message for the whole world?

Pentecost is one of the great Jewish festivals. On that day, seven weeks after Jesus rose from the grave, people from many nations had come to Jerusalem for the celebrations. The followers of Jesus were a small, frightened group in hiding.

'Suddenly there was a noise from the sky which sounded like a strong wind blowing . . . then they saw what looked like tongues of fire which spread out and touched each person there. They were all filled with the Holy Spirit.' A large international crowd gathered, and '. . . they were all excited, because each one of them heard the believers speaking in his own language.'

The result of these remarkable happenings was that three thousand people came to believe in Jesus as the Messiah risen from the grave. And the Christian church as an international community was born.

All this sprang from the believers being 'filled with the Holy Spirit'.

Who is the Holy Spirit?
• The Holy Spirit is God's unseen but personal power. The Spirit led the ancient prophets to prophesy. The Spirit guided the kings of Israel and famous people in Old

Testament days. But he was not for the likes of you and me.

• There are hints in the Old Testament that one day all this will change. God will send his great deliverer and 'the Spirit of the Lord shall rest upon him'.

• That is what happened with Jesus. He was able to fulfil the ancient prophecy:

'The Sovereign Lord has filled me with his spirit. He has chosen me and sent me to bring good news to the poor, to heal the broken-hearted, to announce release to captives and freedom to those in prison.'

He was the only person who had ever been permanently filled by God's Holy Spirit. And so he was uniquely qualified to pass that Spirit on to others.

Things were now very different from Old Testament days. The Holy Spirit was personalized – Jesus in Spirit form. And he was permanently available – for any who would have him.

On the night before he died, Jesus said something that surprised his disciples:

'It is better for you that I go away, because if I do not go, the Helper will not come to you.'

They could not understand this and were very sad.

But he was right.

While he was confined to one human body, he could only relate to a few of them at any one time and in any one place. But once set free from the limitations of a human body, he could relate to anyone, anywhere, at any time. That was much better.

So that is why the physical presence of Jesus was removed from this earth. Instead he sent his 'other self', his Holy Spirit.

When Jesus Christ was raised from the grave, it showed conclusively that death could not remove him from the world. He is alive continually, and can be known by people in all ages.

Through the Holy Spirit his wonderful presence is with everyone who believes in him.

This is why those believers we read of in the New Testament were such burning men. They set the world on fire, and changed the course of history – not by their own brilliance, but by the power of God's Holy Spirit.

A BOOK TO LIVE BY

They called themselves 'followers of the Way'. 'Christians' was a nickname others gave them. And the followers of the Way were notable for their map.

Christians have always been people of the book. That book is of course the Bible. The early believers had only the Old Testament, but they prized it greatly. It was the story of how God had rescued a people and prepared them for himself. More, it contained God's Word, his message to his

Forming principles and choosing right from wrong, we all need God's 'map', the Bible, to guide us through life.

people. It embodied God's Law. Supremely, it pointed forward to God's Son.

Like all Jews, the first Christians were clear that God had revealed himself in that book. They were clear that Jesus was the climax and crown of the gradual unfolding of God's revelation in the Old Testament. So wherever they went they used the Old Testament writings to explain who Jesus was and what he had achieved.

The Old Testament was the root, and Jesus was the fruit, of God's plan to reveal himself to humanity.

Very soon the earliest Christian missionaries were carrying with them copies of the words of Jesus, and the stories of his wonderful life, death and resurrection. Naturally, these began to be set alongside the sacred books of the Old Testament. And so did the writings of his closest followers. He had called them apostles – 'men with mission' – and their task was to draw out for future generations the meaning of his teaching, his life, his death.

Within a comparatively short time the Gospels and letters of the New Testament had been combined with the Old Testament as the book for believers. As Augustine, a church leader at the turn of the fourth century, put it, 'the Christ who is concealed in the Old Testament is revealed in the New'.

They were people of the book.

But there was nothing rigid about this. They did not treat the Bible like the rule book of some trades union. It was a living book.

It is not merely superb literature. It is not merely a source book for Christian beliefs. It is not a lucky dip where any verse can be squeezed to fit any situation.

The Bible is a map.
- It is a guide for the Christian community as they travel through this life.
- It is a library, full of poetry, history, letters and the like.
- It is designed by God to give us enough information to live a joyful, useful, upright and loving life in this world. It is a map, with guidelines, warnings, examples, teaching, encouragement.

But it is no flat, two-dimensional chart. Because through the Bible the living God speaks to those who are prepared to listen humbly and obey what they hear. That example to follow, that warning to heed, that promise to encourage, suddenly springs from the page and speaks to us personally. That is why Christians read it . . . privately . . . in church . . . in group study . . .

It is a book to live by. Through it, the risen Lord gives direction to his people.

A WORLDWIDE COMMUNITY

'Go to all peoples everywhere and make them my disciples.'

'When the Holy Spirit comes upon you, you will be filled with power, and you will be witnesses for me in Jerusalem, in all Judea and Samaria, and to the ends of the earth.'

That is what Jesus had told his followers.

And that is precisely what they did.

In the first three hundred years the Christian faith spread throughout the Roman world, based round the Mediterranean Sea. It reached North Africa, Spain, Germany, France, Yugoslavia, Greece and Turkey.

By the end of the nineteenth century the Christian faith had spread literally throughout the world. You will find Christian communities everywhere from the tribes in the Sahara to the Eskimos near the North Pole.

The church has many different customs in different lands, and widely different forms of organization. But you will always recognize Christians, if they are being true to their Lord and to their calling.

• They share a common faith despite differences of detail: 'one body, one Spirit, one hope, one Lord, one faith, one baptism; there is one God and Father of all mankind.'
• They share a common meal – the Lord's Supper, or Eucharist – in which they remember Jesus' death, draw on the strength of his risen life, and anticipate heaven.
• They keep a special day – Sunday, the day on which

The Christian community, the church, has spread around the world, uniting men and women of many nations and languages.

Jesus rose from the dead. This is a day for rest and worship and re-creation.

Or you could look at it another way. Wherever you find the church loyal to Jesus:
- It will proclaim the teaching and challenge of Jesus.
- It will try to continue the healing ministry of Jesus.
- It will be prepared to share the suffering of Jesus, whether by mockery or by active persecution.
- It will embody something of the joy and power of Jesus.

Of course, the church is made up of sinful, fallible mortals . . . just like us.

So it is not surprising that it makes big mistakes, and at times is very unlike its Master. It does not reckon to have arrived. It is a company on the road.

But in this company you will find guilty people who have found forgiveness through the death of Jesus; lonely people who have discovered the companionship of Jesus; weak people nerved by the power of Jesus' resurrection; fearful people whom his love has made bold. You will find lives in process of change. And you will find a desire to share with others the good news of a Liberator.

Heresy has not entirely ruined them. Apathy has not entirely shrunk them (only in Western Europe is there decline). Persecution has not wiped them out. They continue, and grow, and praise God.

The church is a worldwide community, bringing the love of God to every nation.

A SECULAR SOCIETY?

And what of the world in which Christianity is so widely spread? It is a very different society from the Christian community. It has different assumptions, different goals, different standards.

In the West, society is largely secular. It has come to assume that there is no God, that humanity came from nothing and we are going nowhere beyond ourselves. There is no life after death.

Though not spelt out as baldly as that, such is in fact the basic outlook of most people in secular Western society.

Does it really make any practical difference if the secularists are right, and God is just a cosy dream? The answer lies in the directions society is taking.

It makes a great difference to how we live. If there is no God who has given us rules to live by, why should we not steal – provided we are not found out?

It makes a great difference to our attitude to life. If life is not a gift from God, there is no ultimate argument against euthanasia, abortion, murder and genocide. There is no basic reason why we should not let the hungry starve.

It makes a great difference to the question of meaning and purpose in our lives. If we were not created to know God and enjoy him for ever but are simply the products of biological accident, then there is no good looking for purpose in life. There is none.

It makes a great difference to our attitude to death. These

days death has replaced sex as the subject you never mention. This is hardly surprising if death brings the final extinction of the meaningless ego I call 'myself'.

It makes a great difference to marriage. So long as marriage was seen as a threesome between the partners and the Lord who invented it, there was good reason for couples to stay together. Now there seems to be neither reason nor ability. In some countries one in every two marriages collapses, with appalling results for the partners, the children and the integration of society.

It makes a great difference to our attitude to possessions. Jesus warned people against covetousness. He said, 'A person's true life is not made up of the things he owns, no matter how rich he may be.' Secular society is convinced that a person's life does consist in just that. And so covetousness becomes a way of life.

Christmas is the time when we celebrate God's free gift. But it has become so commercialized that 'grab' has replaced 'give'. Do we want a world where material or where spiritual values count for most?

As a society, we get what we really want . . .

A FAITH EXPLOSION

Drop a stone in a pond, and you will not only disturb the placid surface of the water, you will send ever-widening ripples right across the pond.

That is what happened when the Holy Spirit of Jesus came into the lives of the first disciples on the Day of Pentecost, just fifty days after his resurrection.

It certainly disturbed the placid waters of Judaism. The services were droning on in the temple as usual. Then

In Europe some church buildings stand empty, but in other countries across the world thousands pour into church week by week.

suddenly these men and women were so filled with God's Spirit that they burst out praising him ecstatically in the streets.

Their teaching of a crucified Messiah, risen and able to fill people with his Spirit, disturbed the leaders of Israel. They hoped they had put a stop to this troublesome movement.

Their healing of sick people through the Spirit of Jesus was an equally unwelcome and embarrassing sign of God's power in their lives.

So was the fact that if you put them in prison they would praise God while chained in the stocks, sing hymns at midnight, and bring the gaoler to faith and baptism!

Baptism was the sign or sacrament of the new movement. People were immersed under the water as a mark of the washing away of sins through the death of Jesus, of dying with him and rising to new life through his powerful Spirit inside them. And the evidence in their lives was there for all to see.

The movement spread like wildfire. Perhaps the nearest analogy in nature is the eruption of a volcano. Once, in the middle of the night, I saw Mount Etna in eruption. It was a fantastic sight – a tremendous glare, streams of lava, clouds of steam, and an awesome demonstration of power. It was like that as the Christian movement spread through the nations.

It began among the Jews.

'You have crucified the Messiah (the promised Liberator),' they cried. 'But God has raised him from the dead, and we are witnesses to it.'

And not only in Jerusalem, but throughout the Jewish

homeland of Judea, and even in neighbouring Samaria, men and women in their thousands put their faith in Jesus and discovered the power of his living presence.

It did not stop there. Members of the occupying Roman forces came to the same conclusion and discovered the Holy Spirit was available for them, too. It was the same for complete outsiders, who had looked for ages with longing respect at the religion of Israel. As we have seen on the Day of Pentecost itself, when the whole thing erupted, there were representatives from many nations visiting Jerusalem for the festival. Many of them accepted the Holy Spirit into their own lives.

When a volcano erupts, there is not a lot you can do about it . . .

And wherever its lava spreads, it brings fertility in its wake. Dangerous fertility, of course – you never know when there may be another eruption! But mighty fertile all the same.

Wherever the Holy Spirit has spread down the ages and across the world, there has been a wonderful crop in his wake. A crop of love and unselfishness, of education and medicine, of prisoners liberated, evil habits broken and injustice put right.

The eruption of the Christian volcano is still going on. All over the world people are tasting its power.

WORSHIPPING GOD IN A SELF-CENTRED WORLD

Christians have made their choice.

They want spiritual values to count in their lives. But the pressures of immediate needs, the call of materialism, the rush and stress are still very strong. If we want to live, as the apostle Paul put it, like 'a colony of heaven', it is essential we make time to worship.

'Be still and know that I am God.'

Stillness is essential. Worship is essential. At the heart of the stress there is a deep need to draw aside with God – 'the still point at the centre of the turning world'.

Worship is not escapism. On the contrary it recharges our batteries for living effectively in this world.

Worship is not an optional extra for when I feel like it. However I feel, I need to worship. I am commanded to worship. I cannot survive as a Christian without worship.

Worship literally means 'worth-ship'. We declare by what we say and do that God is worthy to have the supreme place in our lives. And so it goes much deeper than an hour in church once a week.

Christians do worship God in church with others, because we are all members of the same family. We need each other. God has made us interdependent.

We are made in the image of God, yet our lives constantly need to be reshaped to reflect his design.

'Let us not give up the habit of meeting together,' says the New Testament.

Christians also worship God in small groups. All over the world you will find such groups meeting in homes or the open air, in universities and hospitals, in barracks and government buildings. Jesus said, 'Where two or three come together in my name, I am there with them.'

Christians also worship God on their own. Alone on their knees in prayer. Alone with an open Bible. Alone among the glories of nature.

But worship goes even deeper. It involves the whole life. Our bodies and personalities, our gifts and talents, our material possessions and money – all come from God. And Christians want to offer them all back to the Giver for him to use as Jesus would if he was here today.

No wonder worship is the highest possible activity humanity can engage in. It is also the most far-reaching. It affects the whole of life.

Think of a potter at his wheel. Those skilled, strong hands shape the clay as he sees fit. Of course Christians are not just clay. They have wills of their own. But they want to surrender themselves freely and fully to the hands of the Potter, confident that he will mould and use them as he knows best.

That degree of surrender to God, and no less, is worship.

Life no longer pivots on ourselves – but on him.

A LIFESTYLE GOVERNED
BY LOVE

Worship of God and love for others – these are the two great commandments.

'You shall love the Lord your God with all your heart.'

'You shall love your neighbour as yourself.'

Such was Jesus' summary of humanity's whole duty. And he based it on the Old Testament.

When people manage to live like this, it stands out in startling contrast to the selfishness and small-mindedness that are apparent everywhere else. Like a cathedral, it rises above its surroundings. It is beautiful. It is imposing. It needs no justification. A Christian life is like that.

But Christian love is easily misunderstood.

It is not weak and soft. It is not romantic and emotional. It is nothing to do with how we feel.

Christian love is as tough and uncompromising as Jesus Christ. Christian love is as unsentimental as the cross. Christian love is as practical as feeding the hungry, clothing the naked, and bandaging the lepers. The tough early Christian adventurer, Paul, wrote:

'Love is patient and kind; Love is not jealous or conceited or proud; Love is not ill-mannered or selfish or irritable; Love does not keep a record of wrongs; Love is not happy with evil, but is happy with the truth. Love never gives up; and its faith, hope and patience never fail.'

We do not normally grow love like that in the garden of our lives. It is a transplant from God's garden.

'The fruit of the Spirit is love.'

Christians do not love. God loves through them.

An outstanding modern example is Mother Teresa of Calcutta. She does not naturally enjoy being with the smelly, the leprous, the dying. But she is a woman full of the love of Jesus. She loves him so much that she will do anything for him. And that love-relationship with Jesus spills over in a caring love for the destitute dying in the streets of Calcutta.

In us it will take a different form.
- But love, Christian love, always reaches out to the unlovely.
- It always seeks to give rather than to get.
- It is a torch that has been kindled in the fire of God's costly love on the cross.

Love is the greatest thing in the world.

BREAKING THROUGH TO FREEDOM

Jesus Christ saw himself as God's servant, the one described in the Old Testament who would set the captives free.

Captives of every sort.

It is not surprising, therefore, that freedom is one of the leading themes of the New Testament.

'If the Son sets you free, then you really will be free.'

'Am I not a free man? Haven't I seen Jesus our Lord?'

'Freedom is what we have – Christ has set us free! Stand, then, as free people, and do not allow yourselves to become slaves again.'

Often Christians have failed to live up to their charter of freedom. Often the most repressive regimes have come to power in states claiming the name of Christ. But wherever people have been true to Jesus Christ and the teaching of the Bible they have been freedom-fighters.

In the last century, freedom for slaves was bought by Wilberforce and a few others who had a burning Christian faith, and won the day despite fanatical opposition.

Not long afterwards, Shaftesbury's legislation produced decent working conditions for the chimney boys. The Tolpuddle Martyrs led the way for trades unions to protect the rights of workers. These acts of liberation sprang from a living Christian faith.

Today, the fight against illiteracy all over the world is being waged more by Christians than by any other group. Minds are being set free.

Others are caught in the bondage of disease, and it is Christians who are taking the lead in bringing medicine to them in the most undeveloped areas. You do not find hospitals of an atheist foundation in the really primitive areas of the world.

When floods, disease and famine struck Bangladesh, Christians cared. Like Jesus they could not see people trapped in such conditions and remain unaffected. So they did not merely give money. Nurses, plumbers, doctors, builders actually went out to liberate the captives in such a situation – for the most part through Christian agencies and out of love for Jesus.

In South Africa, it is often Christians and churches who are trying to point another way than the road of segregation.

Who are the people who are protesting against Soviet tyranny from within the Soviet Union? Many of them are Christians.

Jesus Christ has declared himself on the side of freedom. He is the Liberator of mankind. And those who loyally follow him are champions of liberation at every level.

LIVING FOR OTHERS IN A SELFISH WORLD

As people in the West look for more sophisticated leisure activities, eating out becomes ever more resplendent. There are even re-creations of medieval banquets – no expense spared.

The contrast with the empty food bowls of the unfortunate is stark and shocking. We feel sorry for the child; we may contribute something to a charity, but then we forget. It is, after all, natural to look after our own interests.

The gap between the rich and the poor countries of the world is widening all the time . . . and the rich countries refuse to do anything to alter the economic arrangements that bring it about. Of course. It is natural to look after our own interests . . .

But Christianity is un-natural. It is supernatural. It is nothing less than the imparting of God's own love to our selfish hearts. When that transfusion takes place, it is bound to make a difference.

'Our love should not be just words and talk; it must be true love, which shows itself in action,' says the apostle John. What does that love look like?
• It makes a difference in lifestyle. Christians will not strive to amass as much money and possessions as they can. They see all they have as belonging to God. They merely administer it. Their home, their money, their material possessions all belong to him. Their homes are open, their giving generous, their eating habits simple, their houses

and possessions unpretentious. At least, they should be . . .

● It makes a difference in home life. In many families, selfishness reigns supreme, with husbands, wives and children all doing their own thing and pressing their own rights. Christians try to take a very different stance. Husband and wife try to outdo each other in love and self-sacrifice . . .

The husband is out to protect his wife from worry and strain, to give himself to her in love and thoughtfulness, and to make any sacrifice for her.

The wife seeks to submit in love to her husband, to be affectionate towards him, to support him – forgetting herself and her 'rights'.

The children aim to obey and honour their parents as they would the Lord – while the parents are careful not to provoke and irritate their children with needless prohibitions.

You will find it all in Paul's letter to the Ephesians. Revolutionary stuff for family living. And the wonder is, it works!

● It makes a difference to industrial relations. All over the West, management and labour see each other as enemies. 'Squeeze all you can from the other side' seems to be the motto. Industrial relations are often the law of the jungle. But how about this teaching from the New Testament?

For management: 'Do the honest thing by your employees, and have done with threats. Remember, both you and they have a Master in heaven.'

For employees: 'Put your back into your work for your earthly employers. Do not skimp the job, hoping it will get by. You are working for the Lord and not just for men.'

Who says Christianity does not make a difference? The love revolution is the greatest power in the world.

It only needs to be tried.

The Bible offers clear, yet revolutionary, principles for industrial relations.

BEYOND THE CREMATORIUM

Wherever the church has been loyal to its Founder, it has been marked by love, self-sacrifice and freedom. But the church does not believe God's kingdom can be brought in by human effort. Christians work for the improvement of this world as if there were no other. But they are only strengthened to do so because there *is* another.

Death is not the end.

The Christian hope of life after death is not based on the idea that the human soul is naturally immortal. No, Christians believe that eternal life, like everything else in Christianity, is a gift from the generous God who has set us free.

'God's free gift is eternal life in union with Christ Jesus our Lord.'

Even if there were no life after death, I would rather be a Christian than an atheist. I am not aware that I am moved by a desire to continue existing for ever. It is enough for me to know the love and forgiveness and joy of the Lord here and now.

But he has said that he will not scrap me at death.

His people are too precious to him.

So he has devised a transformation that will take them from this life to the next. The next life will be spent with him and his people for ever in the new dimension called heaven.

Nature gives a wonderful illustration of what life after death will be like. The Swallowtail caterpillar is not a particularly beautiful beast. Not very mobile. Only interested in eating . . .

But the caterpillar comes to a stage when its caterpillar life must end. It grows disinterested in eating. It becomes restless. It spins itself a cocoon, and turns into a chrysalis. To all intents and purposes it is dead.

But really it is very far from dead. That caterpillar existence is transformed into the totally new dimension of living enjoyed by the butterfly. And the Swallowtail butterfly is extremely beautiful. It is highly mobile. It is interested in flowers and sunshine. It soars high among the trees . . .

So it is with Christians after death. Here on earth we are not very beautiful creatures, despite the grace of God at work in us. Often we are selfish, earthbound in our interests. There is something restless about us.

But when we die, that is not the end of us. We emerge into the sunshine of God's home – the same people we were on earth, only wonderfully transformed. The caterpillar has turned into a full butterfly. No longer selfish. No longer earthbound. But free to enjoy the totally new dimension of existence beyond the grave.

There is nothing materialistic about all this. Heaven, as the Bible describes it, is not a place of sensuous delights. It is an utterly different quality of experience. Heaven is to earth what the world of the butterfly is to the world of the caterpillar.

No self-respecting caterpillar is enthusiastic about ending his days in a cocoon . . .

But no self-respecting butterfly would want to go back to being a caterpillar again . . .

'To leave this life and be with Christ is a far better thing.'

What happens after death? Christianity claims that like a butterfly emerging from its chrysalis we will enter into a new life.